THE RIDDLER (Illustrated):

300 OF THE BEST RIDDLES SMART KIDS A

BY

Sebastian Carpenter

Also in the series…

150 CHALLENGING MATHEMATHICS RIDDLES & BRAIN TEASERS TO SHARPEN YOUR BRAIN

THE MATH RIDDLER

- Illustrated -

Sebastian Carpenter

TABLE OF CONTENTS

Preface

Chapter 1: Troublesome Riddles

Chapter 2: Tricky Riddles

Chapter 3: Formidable Riddles

Preface

With the emergence of the internet and in a world where our lives are becoming ever more engrossed in social media, it is extremely important to find ways to learn and develop outside of these areas. For people to succeed in making the world a better place, it's essential for them to possess the ability to distinguish between that what can cause harm and that what causes human beings to flourish. Experts throughout the ages have recommended riddles for people as something to stretch their minds and improve their ability to think and be creative. Riddles aid development in problem-solving skills for kids and people of all ages, and we're not talking about literal "problems" such as ones faced at school or at the workplace.

Why is problem-solving important?

Riddles and brainteasers make our brain work in an interesting way. Our neural network constantly connects and reconnects in a never-ending number of ways and in pursuit of pinning down a specific solution. They trigger millions of neural connections that stimulate the reasoning part of your intellect.

Our "logical reasoning" is also tested when we solve riddles. Working in a direction with tangible, measurable and attainable time-bounded obstacles bends our mind toward a more efficient logical approach which stays with us into adulthood and applies to our everyday life. Logical stimulation enables us to see things from a different perspective to that which we might have ordinarily chosen out of routine.

Most of the riddles are short, precise and easy to read and understand. Therefore as you grapple with possible answers, you're showing yet another part of growth. You will be locating answers and applying cognitive practices.

How do you encourage problem-solving?

As an educator or parent it is important for you to know how to work with your children to advance their problem-solving skills. After all, your kids will have to use these skills both at school and at home. You can help your kids to find the answers. Aid them in figuring out exactly what the issue is. Then, brainstorm possible solutions together. Further, practice reading together often. You can role-play by choosing your child's favourite character and asking them how they would work out the problem. Encourage them to be creative. There's nothing wrong with some guidance. However, try not to worry about whether their answers are correct. Finally, be sure to surround the kids in an environment that will also cultivate their personal growth.

For adults, riddles are a proven way to enhance the functionality of your brain. They have a long lasting and profound effect on the power of our brains. Solving them on daily basis can be great mind-exercise. Not only do they sharpen our memory but also the logical reasoning of our brain.

How do you teach riddles?

Children need to read a lot to boost their vocabulary. This comes from constant practice.

Riddles are an excellent method to enhance their vocabulary. When you're also sharing and solving riddles with children, it gives them a chance to bond with you. Also, it helps them to get out of their comfort zone and mix with others.

Once our brain starts extracting inferences from what's in front of us, we possess the ability to enjoy life on a new level; not only logically but emotionally too. With the clear thinking that you will obtain from the challenges laid out by those riddles, you will gain the knowledge and solutions at the back of your mind and a reinvigorated virtue, to tackle every new day with intellect. Most importantly, growth and development milestones can literally be considered as the foundation of our lives.

Chapter 1: Troublesome Riddles

These riddles are fast-paced, short and a tad easier to comprehend. They are a great way to introduce you to the challenges contained within this book and to the wonderful universe of riddles.

1. I am something to make you think, I am something to make you know. I am something to which the answer you might never know.

   Annotation: You are searching for the answer to one right now.

2. Four legs up, four legs down, soft in the middle and hard all around.

   Annotation: Lay your head down.

3. I am so simple, that I can only point yet I guide men all over the world!

   Annotation: I'm circular.

4. If you feed it, it lives. If you water it-it dies!

   Annotation: I burn brightly.

5. What has legs but cannot walk?

   Annotation: It's sturdy.

6. What gets more wet as it dries?

   Annotation: Wrap yourself up in this.

7. It occurs once in a minute, twice in a moment, but never in an hour.

   Annotation: The alphabet.

8. What stinks when living and smells good when dead?

   Annotation: Find it on a farm.

9.   I have keys but no doors, I have space but no rooms, I allow you to enter but you are never able to leave. What am I?

Annotation: Press me.

10.   I have wings, I am able to fly, I'm not a bird yet I soar high in the sky. What am I?

Annotation: I sell treats too.

11.   I am a fruit, I am a bird and I am also a person. What am I?

Annotation: I taste good in green.

12.   What is often on the ground getting stepped on by others, but you don't have to wash it because it never gets dirty, in fact you couldn't wash it even if you tried?

Annotation: Find it more often in summer.

13.   What has feet on the inside but not on the outside?

Annotation: They can smell.

14.   When does April come before January?

Annotation: You look inside it.

15.   What do Taylor Swift and an air conditioner have in common?

Annotation: They cheer for you.

FIND THE ANSWERS ON THE NEXT PAGE!

1. Riddle.
2. Bed.
3. Compass.
4. Fire.
5. Table.
6. Towel.
7. The letter "M".
8. Pig (oink oink)
9. Keyboard.
10. Airplane.
11. Kiwi.
12. Shadow.
13. Shoes.
14. In the dictionary.
15. They both have fans.

16.   When can you eat, play with, watch with and listen to music on?

Annotation: It's famous worldwide.

17.   What do autumn, Halloween, August, and Dracula have in common that a pumpkin doesn't have?

Annotation: Think about it!

18.   Four rubber ducks were floating in the bathtub, two floated away and two drowned. How many ducks are still alive?

Annotation: Do rubber ducks need air?

19.   I can run fast and slow, I can be high or low. I can slip through almost anything, and I am needed by the poor and even kings. What am I?

Annotation: I'm an odorless substance.

20.   You keep me close to you and you save me no matter how small or big and dirty I get. What am I?

Annotation: It makes the world go around.

21.   Which weighs more: a ton of concrete or a ton of feathers?

Annotation: Look closely!

22.   A purple and orange dead butterfly is in the middle of a spider web and all of its legs are caught in the web. The spider notices it and comes running at it ready to tie it up and consume it. If the butterfly wants to get away from a spider, would it have the best chance of survival if it fluttered its wings, wiggled its legs or did both?

Annotation: What state is the butterfly currently in?

23. A doctor and a boy were fishing. The boy was the doctor's son, but the doctor was not the boy's father. Who was the doctor?

    Annotation: A relation.

24. What belongs to you, but is used more by others?

    Annotation: Everybody has one.

25. What is something you can keep in your pocket that keeps it empty?

    Annotation: You will sometimes find one in your pocket.

26. How many animals did Moses take on the ark?

    Annotation: Who went on the ark again?

27. If six children and two dogs weren't under an umbrella, how come none of them got wet?

    Annotation: What's the weather like again?

28. What begins with the letter 't', is full of 't' and finishes with 't'.

    Annotation: The part that goes inside was discovered in Ancient China.

29. In a single-story house, there is a red chair, red bed, red computer, red flowers, red table, and a red carpet. Everything around is a red colour. What colour is the staircase?

    Annotation: Levels.

30.   I have a face and two hands, but no arms or legs. What am I?

Annotation: Look on the wall.

**FIND THE ANSWERS
ON THE
NEXT PAGE!**

16. Apple.
17. The letter "A".
18. Zero, because rubber ducks aren't alive and cannot drown.
19. Water.
20. Money.
21. They both weigh exactly the same, one ton.
22. The butterfly can't do any of those things because it's dead.
23. His mother.
24. Your name.
25. A big hole.
26. Moses didn't take any animals on the ark. Noah did!
27. Because it wasn't raining.
28. A teapot with tea in it.
29. It's a single-storey house, there is no staircase.
30. Clock.

31. Why can't a man living in New York be buried in Chicago?

    Annotation: Breath.

32. What needs to be broken before you use it?

    Annotation: I hatch too.

33. Tommy throws the ball as hard as he can, and it comes back to him, without anything or anybody touching it. How?

    Annotation: The clouds.

34. What has holes all over, but still holds water?

    Annotation: I inspired a famous square cartoon character.

35. A boy fell off a forty foot ladder, but still did not get hurt. Why?

    Annotation: How high?

36. Which tree can be carried in your hand?

    Annotation: Tropical climates.

37. What has a horn but doesn't make any noise?

    Annotation: Find it in Africa.

38. You can serve it, but cannot eat it?

    Annotation: Wimbledon.

39. I am brought for eating, but people don't eat me. Why?

Annotation: In Greece, they smash them.

40. A teddy bear is always full. Why?

Annotation: A synonym of full.

41. Three men jump into the water, but only two come out with wet hair. Why?

Annotation: An eagle.

42. If you are travelling south on an electric train, which way is the smoke from the train going?

Annotation: Coal.

43. They come at night without being called and disappear during the day without being stolen. What are they?

Annotation: The sun.

44. What has one eye but can't see?

Annotation: Sewing.

45. There is a special kind of fish that can never swim. What is it?

Annotation: Tombstone.

46. I'm the most slippery country in the world. What am I?

Annotation: I'm in Europe.

47. What stays where it is and goes off?

    Annotation: Set me daily.

48. I don't have eyes, ears, a nose or tongue. But I can see, smell and taste everything. What am I?

    Annotation: Think with it.

49. What building has more and more stories than any book?

    Annotation: Use your card.

50. What goes up and down but never moves?

    Annotation: People can have one too.

FIND THE ANSWERS
ON THE
NEXT PAGE!

31. Because he's alive.
32. Egg.
33. He threw it upwards.
34. Sponge.
35. He fell off the bottom step.
36. Palm tree.
37. Rhinoceros.
38. Tennis ball.
39. Because I'm a plate.
40. Because it is stuffed.
41. The third man was bald.
42. Nowhere. An electric train doesn't produce smoke.
43. Stars.
44. Needle.
45. Dead fish.
46. Greece.
47. Alarm clock.
48. Brain.
49. Library.
50. Temperature.

51. The more you take, the more you leave behind. What are they?

    Annotation: There are lots of different sizes.

52. A yellow house is made out of yellow bricks and a red house is made out of red bricks – so what is a greenhouse made up of?

    Annotation: I'm transparent.

53. The more you have of it, the less you see. What is it?

    Annotation: Vincent van Gogh loved it.

54. Mr. Black lives in a black house, Mr. Brown lives in the brown house, and Mr. Green lives in the green house. Who do you think lives in the white house?

    Annotation: The first letter begins with "P".

55. The one who made it didn't want it, the one who bought it didn't want it. The one who used it never saw it? What is it?

    Annotation: Underground.

56. It is just something that everyone does at the same time. What is it?

    Annotation: Animals do it too.

57. It can fill a room without occupying any space. What is it?

    Annotation: It travels fast.

58. What is so fragile that saying its name breaks it?

Annotation: It's golden.

59. What is it easy to get into and hard to get out of?

Annotation: It happens to everybody.

60. After a train crashed, every single person died. Who survived?

Annotation: They're in it together.

61. What travels around the world but stays in one spot?

Annotation: Get me from the Post Office.

62. What is always in front of you but can't be seen?

Annotation: Fortune tellers.

63. Where can you find cities, towns, shops, and streets but no people?

Annotation: Nowadays people check Google for it.

64. I am full of keys, but I cannot open any door. What am I?

Annotation: Play me.

65. It lives in winter, dies in summer, and grows with its roots on top. What is it?

Annotation: I appear when it's freezing.

FIND THE ANSWERS
ON THE
NEXT PAGE!

51. Footsteps.
52. Glass.
53. Paint.
54. The President.
55. Coffin.
56. Grow older.
57. Light.
58. Silence.
59. Trouble.
60. All of the couples.
61. Stamp.
62. Future.
63. Maps..
64. Piano.
65. Icicle.

66. I have three letters. I read the same backward and forward. You use me all the time, but the irony is that you do not see me. What am I?

    Annotation: I come in different colours.

67. I am as light as air, but you cannot hold or lift me. What am I?

    Annotation: You want me in your bath.

68. I fly around the entire day yet I never go to a new place. What am I?

    Annotation: Every nation has one.

69. I have teeth, but I don't eat. What am I?

    Annotation: Use me before you go to school or work.

70. Where do fish keep their money?

    Annotation: The side of the river.

71. Poke your fingers in my eyes and I will open my mouth wide. What am I?

    Annotation: I'm an enemy of paper.

72. I do not exist now but eventually, come to existence. People know that I exist, but when I arrive I change my name. I motivate people and give them hope. What am I?

    Annotation: Look into the future.

73. I can be long, or I can be short. I can be grown, and I can be bought. I can

be painted, or I can be left bare. I can be round, I can even be square. What am I?

Annotation: I'm always with you.

74. You can hear me, but you can't see me, and I won't answer unless spoken to. What am I?

Annotation: I'm even louder in tunnels.

75. It can be cracked, it can be made, it can be told, it can be played. What is it?

Annotation: I'm funny.

76. If you blow past your destination, you'll have to throw your car into this.

Annotation: Look behind you.

77. I go around the yard, but I do not move. What am I?

Annotation: I can be painted too.

78. When things go wrong, what can you always count on?

Annotation: They are long.

79. It is black when you purchase it but becomes red when you use it, and then grey when you dispose of it. What is it?

Annotation: Trains use it.

80. How can you make seven even?

Annotation: Letters.

FIND THE ANSWERS
ON THE
NEXT PAGE!

66. Eye.
67. Bubbles.
68. Flag.
69. Comb.
70. Riverbank.
71. Scissors.
72. Tomorrow.
73. Fingernail.
74. Echo.
75. Jokes.
76. Reverse.
77. Fence.
78. Your fingers.
79. Coal.
80. Take away the "S".

81. What has a ring, but no finger?

    Annotation: You hold me.

82. What can you break without touching it?

    Annotation: The word "pinky" sometimes precedes it.

83. What word has five letters but sounds like it only has one?

    Annotation: You wait in one.

84. I will lose my head in the mornings, but I will gain it again at night! What am I?

    Annotation: I'm soft.

85. My best buddy always makes mistakes. But I would easily get rid of the mistakes. What am I?

    Annotation: Find me in your pencil case.

86. I am a nut with a hole? What am I?

    Annotation: Top me off with icing.

87. I may seem real, but it always turns out I was only there in your sleep. What am I?

    Annotation: I can be fun or scary.

88. What is big and yellow and comes in the morning, to brighten mom's

day?

Annotation: Kids get on it.

89. What is the longest word in the dictionary?

    Annotation: Run for…

90. A man rode into town on Tuesday and stayed in a hotel. Two nights later he rode home on Tuesday. How?

    Annotation: Saddle up.

91. What can run but can't walk?

    Annotation: You need me to survive.

92. What has a bottom at the top?

    Annotation: They come in pairs.

93. I have a straight back and sharp teeth for cutting. What am I?

    Annotation: Use me on wood.

94. It always stays hot even when put in the refrigerator.

    Annotation: I'm a vegetable.

95. Drop me from the tallest building and I will survive. Drop me from the smallest of boats and I will be destroyed. What am I?

    Annotation: I begin as wood.

96. Why is the ocean so friendly?

Annotation: Surfers enjoy them.

97. They have no flesh nor feathers nor scales nor bones. Yet they have fingers and thumbs of their own. What are they?

    Annotation: They are useful in the winter.

98. What common English verb becomes its own past tense by rearranging its letters?

    Annotation: People do it daily.

99. What can you catch but not throw?

    Annotation: Splutter, splutter.

00. It only has two bones, but there are thousands of ribs. What is it?

    Annotation: Choo, choo.

FIND THE ANSWERS ON THE NEXT PAGE!

81. Phone.
82. Promise.
83. Queue.
84. Pillow.
85. Eraser.
86. Donut.
87. Dreams.
88. School bus.
89. Smiles! There is a mile between each "s".
90. Tuesday is the name of his horse.
91. Water.
92. Legs.
93. Saw.
94. Pepper.
95. Paper.
96. Because it always waves.
97. Gloves.
98. Eat.
99. A cold.
100. Railway track.

Chapter 2: Tricky Riddles

These riddles are concise, yet pesky and a step-up in level regarding understanding. Good luck finding a solution to the second stage of these brain teasers.

101. It takes twelve men twelve hours to construct a wall. Then how long will it take six men to complete the same wall?

    Annotation: Read it over and over.

102. He always drives a customer away? Who is he?

    Annotation: In New York City, they're all yellow.

103. It always becomes white when it becomes dirty. What is it?

    Annotation: It's used in school.

104. I sit on a bridge and people see the world through me. I can add colour to the world and perhaps make you look good. What am I?

    Annotation: Police

105. I am alive without breath and as cold as death. I am never thirsty but always drinking. What am I?

    Annotation: I have scales too.

106. I have three eyes but only one leg. I still close one even if you beg. What am I?

    Annotation: In South Africa they call me a robot.

107. I use a long track. I transport heavy loads. Many tourists use me. Watch lights stop for me. I will show you beautiful scenery.

    Annotation: I begin with a T.

108. There is a rooster sitting on top of a barn. If it laid an egg, which way would it roll?

Annotation: Gender.

109. How many months have twenty-eight days?

Annotation: Count them.

110. What's black and white and read all over?

Annotation: I'm sometimes delivered to your door.

111. What has four wheels and flies?

Annotation: I smell bad.

112. What has a bed but never sleeps, can run but never walk, and has a bank but no money?

Annotation: I flow.

113. Who can shave twenty-five times a day but still have a beard?

Annotation: You visit them a few times each year.

114. All about the house, with his lady he dances, yet he always works and never romances.

Annotation: Witches love me.

115. Brothers and sisters I have none but that man's father is my father's son.

Annotation: I'm a place for vanity.

FIND THE ANSWERS
ON THE
NEXT PAGE!

101. No time! The wall has already been constructed.
102. Taxi driver.
103. Blackboard.
104. Sunglasses.
105. Fish.
106. Traffic light
107. Train.
108. Roosters don't lay eggs.
109. All of them.
110. Newspaper.
111. Garbage truck.
112. River.
113. Barber.
114. Broomstick.
115. Looking at yourself in the mirror.

2020 Calendar

January

Su	Mo	Tu	We	Th	Fr	Sa
29	30	31	1	2	3	4
5	6	7	8	9	10	11
12	13	14	15	16	17	18
19	20	21	22	23	24	25
26	27	28	29	30	31	

February

Su	Mo	Tu	We	Th	Fr	Sa
26	27	28	29	30	31	1
2	3	4	5	6	7	8
9	10	11	12	13	14	15
16	17	18	19	20	21	22
23	24	25	26	27	28	29

March

Su	Mo	Tu	We	Th	Fr	Sa
1	2	3	4	5	6	7
8	9	10	11	12	13	14
15	16	17	18	19	20	21
22	23	24	25	26	27	28
29	30	31	1	2	3	4

April

Su	Mo	Tu	We	Th	Fr	Sa
29	30	31	1	2	3	4
5	6	7	8	9	10	11
12	13	14	15	16	17	18
19	20	21	22	23	24	25
26	27	28	29	30	1	2

May

Su	Mo	Tu	We	Th	Fr	Sa
26	27	28	29	30	1	2
3	4	5	6	7	8	9
10	11	12	13	14	15	16
17	18	19	20	21	22	23
24	25	26	27	28	29	30
31	1	2	3	4	5	6

June

Su	Mo	Tu	We	Th	Fr	Sa
31	1	2	3	4	5	6
7	8	9	10	11	12	13
14	15	16	17	18	19	20
21	22	23	24	25	26	27
28	29	30	1	2	3	4

July

Su	Mo	Tu	We	Th	Fr	Sa
28	29	30	1	2	3	4
5	6	7	8	9	10	11
12	13	14	15	16	17	18
19	20	21	22	23	24	25
26	27	28	29	30	31	

August

Su	Mo	Tu	We	Th	Fr	Sa
26	27	28	29	30	31	1
2	3	4	5	6	7	8
9	10	11	12	13	14	15
16	17	18	19	20	21	22
23	24	25	26	27	28	29
30	31	1	2	3	4	5

September

Su	Mo	Tu	We	Th	Fr	Sa
30	31	1	2	3	4	5
6	7	8	9	10	11	12
13	14	15	16	17	18	19
20	21	22	23	24	25	26
27	28	29	30	1	2	3

October

Su	Mo	Tu	We	Th	Fr	Sa
27	28	29	30	1	2	3
4	5	6	7	8	9	10
11	12	13	14	15	16	17
18	19	20	21	22	23	24
25	26	27	28	29	30	31

November

Su	Mo	Tu	We	Th	Fr	Sa
1	2	3	4	5	6	7
8	9	10	11	12	13	14
15	16	17	18	19	20	21
22	23	24	25	26	27	28
29	30	1	2	3	4	5

December

Su	Mo	Tu	We	Th	Fr	Sa
29	30	1	2	3	4	5
6	7	8	9	10	11	12
13	14	15	16	17	18	19
20	21	22	23	24	25	26
27	28	29	30	31	1	2

116.   A box without hinges, key, or lid yet golden treasure inside is hid. What am I?

Annotation: I sometimes take shape in chocolate.

117.   I am a precious little thing, dancing and eating all the time. Watch me from a distance, so you can feel my warm and gentle love. But don't come to close or my next meal you could be. What am I?

Annotation: I'm an element.

118.   Come up and we go. Go down and we stay.

Annotation: Docking.

119.   It goes up and down without moving.

Annotation: It serves royalty in red.

120.   I know a word of letters three, add two and less there will be.

Annotation: Not many.

121.   I can be written, I can be spoken, I can be exposed, I can be broken.

Annotation: I'm uploaded daily.

122.   I run, yet I have no legs. What am I?

Annotation: Poke it unwantedly.

123.   Dead on the field ten soldiers lie in white, felled by three eyes, black as night. What happened?

44

Annotation: Change your shoes before you start.

24.   I am the outstretched fingers that seize and hold the wind. Wisdom flows from me in other hands. Upon me are sweet dreams dreamt. And my merest touch brings laughter. What am I?

Annotation: Find me on a hat.

25.   Take one out and scratch my head I am now black but once I was red.

Annotation: Find me in a box.

26.   A house of wood in a hidden place. Built without nails or glue. High above the earthen ground it holds pale gems of blue.

Annotation: I provide shelter.

27.   What is the one thing that all wise men, regardless of their religion or politics, agree is between heaven and earth? What is it?

Annotation: I'm used to connect.

28.   It occurs once in a minute, twice in a moment, but never in an hour.

Annotation: It's not a thing.

29.   Is it legal for a man to marry his widow's sister?

Annotation: Read carefully.

30.   When is a door not a door?

Annotation: Find jam in it.

FIND THE ANSWERS
ON THE
NEXT PAGE!

116. Egg.
117. Fire.
118. Anchor.
119. Carpet.
120. Few.
121. News.
122. Nose.
123. A bowling ball knocked down ten pins.
124. Feather.
125. A match.
126. Nest.
127. The word "and".
128. The letter "M".
129. No because he's dead.
130. When it's ajar.

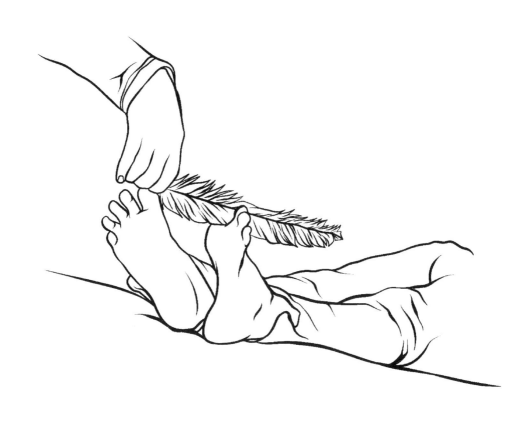

31. Squeeze it and it cries tears as red as it's flesh. It's heart is made of stone.

     Annotation: Find me at the peak of treats.

32. I come out of the earth, I am sold in the market. He who buys me cuts off the tail, takes off my suit of silk, and weeps beside me when I'm dead.

     Annotation: Layers.

33. I touch your face. I'm in your words, I'm lack of space and beloved by birds.

     Annotation: I'm crucial to life.

34. Large as a mountain, small as a pea. Endlessly swimming in a waterless sea.

     Annotation: I begin with an A.

35. What breaks but never falls?

     Annotation: I'm also a name for a girl.

36. What has roots as nobody sees, is taller than trees. Up, up it goes. And yet never grows?

     Annotation: I stretch across countries.

37. What can be quick and deadly and gathers by the ocean?

     Annotation: I'm very fine.

38. What can you hold in your left hand and not in your right?

Annotation: Hit me I'm funny.

139. A monkey, a squirrel, and a bird are racing to the top of a coconut tree. Who will get the banana first, the monkey, the squirrel, or the bird?

    Annotation: Where do I grow again?

140. What room do ghosts avoid?

    Annotation: I'm alive in name.

141. Your parents come over for a surprise breakfast while you are sleeping. You get out pancakes, toast, maple syrup and jam. What do you open first?

    Annotation: You need them functioning before you do any of this.

142. With shiny fangs, my bloodless bite will bring together what's mostly white. What am I?

    Annotation: I bring things together.

143. How many seconds are in a year?

    Annotation: Monthly.

144. Born in an instant. I tell all stories. I can be lost. But I never die? What am I?

    Annotation: They can revisit you at any time.

145. I am the reason you run. I am the reason you scream. I am the cause of your pain. I am a cage from which you will never be free.

    Annotation: Feed me well and keep me healthy.

46. What word in the English language does the following: the first two letters signify a male, the first three letters signify a female, the first four letter signify a great, while the entire word signifies a great woman. What is the word?

Annotation: I start with a H and end with an E.

47. It's shorter than the rest, but when you're happy, you raise it up like it's the best. What is it?

Annotation: It's Tom's surname in famous folklore.

48. What do people spend a lot of money on every year but never want to use it?

Annotation: I make your car and house more secure.

49. Ambitious people will climb the social version of contraption. What is it?

Annotation: I reach heights.

50. It's a home in the air. What is it?

Annotation: I spread out over cities.

FIND THE ANSWERS
ON THE
NEXT PAGE!

131. Cherry.
132. Onion.
133. Air.
134. Asteroids.
135. Dawn.
136. Mountains.
137. Sand.
138. Your right elbow.
139. None of them, because you can't get a banana from a coconut tree.
140. Living room.
141. Your eyes.
142. Stapler.
143. Twelve of them: January 2nd, February 2nd, etc.
144. Memories.
145. Your body.
146. Heroine.
147. Thumb.
148. Insurance.
149. Ladder.
150. Apartment.

151. Take it and you will lose or gain more than all the others.

    Annotation: I can be both dangerous and prosperous.

152. Pirates put their goodies in it. What is it?

    Annotation: I'm also part of the human anatomy.

153. Once they sailed the sea, now they surf the internet.

    Annotation: Blackbeard is one of the most famous ones.

154. A sphere has three, a circle has two, and a point has zero. What is it?

    Annotation: I'm measurable.

155. The day is there night and the night is there day, when I shout and they shout back I run away.

    Annotation: I'm the number one fear of a famous superhero.

156. What do cheetahs, dalmatians and appaloosas have in common?

    Annotation: Humans get them on their face too.

157. I can the trees my home, yet I never go inside, and if I ever fall off the tree I will be surely dead.

    Annotation: I decompose in time.

158. What do roses, chocolates, laces, love knots, the colour red and hearts have in common?

Annotation: A special day for couples.

159. Sometimes imaginary and sometimes real, sometimes they are the closes and dearest person outside the family. Who are they?

Annotation: They can last for a lifetime.

160. Round and round I go never stopping in a continuous flow. I hang out with numbers each and every day and nothing ever gets on my way. Wha am I?

Annotation: There are two of me.

161. Sally, Lisa and Bernadette are triplets. But Sally and Lisa share something that Bernadette does not. What is it?

Annotation: What's missing?

162. Break it and it gets better, immediately set and harder to break again.

Annotation: Usain Bolt loves them.

163. What kind of apple isn't an apple?

Annotation: You can eat rice out of me in Thailand.

164. What tyre doesn't move when the car turns right?

Annotation: It shares a name with a half strike in ten-pin bowling.

165. What is yellow, looks like the moon and has seeds.

Annotation: I grow in tropical countries.

FIND THE ANSWERS
ON THE
NEXT PAGE!

151.   Risk.
152.   Chest.
153.   Pirates.
154.   Dimensions.
155.   Bats.
156.   Spots.
157.   Leaves.
158.   They are all symbols of Valentine's Day.
159.   Friends.
160.   The hands of a clock.
161.   The letter "L" in their names.
162.   Record.
163.   Pineapple.
164.   Spare tire.
165.   Bananas.

166. Which one of Santa's reindeer can be seen on Valentine's day?

     Annotation: I carry a bow and arrow.

167. If you spot one of these eastern warriors, they're not doing their job right.

     Annotation: They're Japanese.

168. There is a woman on a boat, on a lake, wearing a coat. If you want to know her name, it's in the riddle I just wrote. What's the woman's name.

     Annotation: Look carefully.

169. In what year did Christmas Day and New Year's Day fall in the same year?

     Annotation: Was there just one year in particular?

170. What comes with your car, but travels more than your car?

     Annotation: Start it up.

171. What has roots and can be white and yellow at the same time?
     Annotation: They yank me out when I'm causing trouble.

172. What has no hands but might knock on your door, and if it does you better open up?

     Annotation: I begin with the letter O.

173. What gets colder as it warms up?

     Annotation: I'm required in summer.

74. The eight of us go forth not back to protect our king from a foes attack.

    Annotation: Find me in black or white.

75. Who has married hundreds but has always been single?

    Annotation: I'm ordained.

76. What was the first man made invention that can see through a wall?

    Annotation: If I shatter don't pick me up with your bare hands.

77. How do you spell hard water with only three letters?

    Annotation: I can help you when you sprain your ankle.

78. Deep, deep, do they go. Spreading out as they go. Never needing any air. They are sometimes as fine as hair.

    Annotation: I begin with an R.

79. What can't you find in European countries like Spain, Germany and France that you'll find in Asian countries like Brunei, Papa New Guinea and Bhutan?

    Annotation: I'm not an object.

80. An art-form and its colour-ful result. What am I?

    Annotation: Many famous people have created me.

FIND THE ANSWERS ON THE NEXT PAGE!

166. Cupid.
167. Ninja.
168. "There" is the woman's name.
169. It happens every year.
170. Keys.
171. Teeth.
172. Opportunity.
173. Air conditioner.
174. Chess pawns.
175. Priest.
176. Window.
177. Ice.
178. Roots.
179. The letter "U".
180. Painting.

81. I have one eye. See near and far. I hold the moments you treasure. And the things that make you weep.

    Annotation: I like to zoom.

82. Lovely and round. I shine with pale light, grown in the darkness, a lady's delight.

    Annotation: They form in oysters.

83. They are the shore's gallant knights.

    Annotation: If a ship has capsized they will appear.

84. It can be used onstage or to express admiration. What is it?

    Annotation: I begin with the letter P.

85. Environmentalists want to keep this from drying. What am I?

    Annotation: I have aquatic plants.

86. I am the red tongue of earth, that buries cities.

    Annotation: I'm molten.

87. What devours all and can kill a king. Destroy a town and crushes mountains.

    Annotation: There is never enough of it in a day.

88. I bring celebrities into your home.

Annotation: I begin in 1927.

189. I am a million people's wakeup call. What am I?

    Annotation: Brazil is my biggest producer.

190. People in love are often bound to this.

    Annotation: Meet me at the altar.

191. I'm the loyalist of companions; I seek your attention wherever you go.

    Annotation: Don't rile me up though.

192. Hearing something unexpected or touching a live wire can have this effect.

    Annotation: I begin with the letter S.

193. Something you carry while singing. What is it?

    Annotation: I'm a melody.

194. What travels from coast to coast without ever moving?

    Annotation: I make places more accessible.

195. Nothing specific, but more than a few. This many clustered, together will do.

    Annotation: A number of things, typically the same thing.

196. I'm a blind superhero. Who am I?

    Annotation: I'm also Evil Knievel's profession.

97. Often wondering the streets, this group of people cannot afford to be choosers.

Annotation: I begin with the letter B.

98. They are toothy nocturnal immortals. Who are they?

Annotation: They inspired the movie franchise "Twilight".

99. I'm a stylish winter top that covers your larynx.

Annotation: I'm named after a slow reptile.

00. We are the group who manage the winged engines of war. What are we?

Annotation: We provide defence.

**FIND THE ANSWERS
ON THE
NEXT PAGE!**

181. Camera.
182. Pearls.
183. Coast Guard.
184. Props.
185. Wetland.
186. Lava.
187. Time.
188. Television.
189. Coffee bean.
190. Marriage.
191. Dog.
192. Shock.
193. Tune.
194. Highway.
195. Bunch.
196. Daredevil.
197. Beggars.
198. Vampires.
199. Turtleneck.
200. Air Force.

Chapter 3: Formidable Riddles

Welcome to the big league. You've made it this far, so now it's time to crack the toughest riddles on this journey.

01. It carries paper of the most important sort but also plastic. I'm glad to report. What is it?

    Annotation: Women use a purse.

02. A prehistoric reptile that lives today and the inspiration for the name of a popular sports drink.

    Annotation: I scour freshwater environments.

03. Whipping out one of these in the wrong setting is said to be bad luck. What am I?

    Annotation: Don't open me indoors.

04. Rotten trees and Jack-O-Lanterns have this characteristic in common. What is it?

    Annotation: Lacking.

05. Men in skirts blow into these. What are they?

    Annotation: Find us in Scotland sporting our tartan.

06. You use it between your head and your toes, the more it works the thinner it grows. What is it?

    Annotation: Dove make it.

07. A man parks his car outside of a hotel and immediately realises he is bankrupt. How did it happen?

    Annotation: Roll the dice.

208. I was born in mire and muck; of velvets and rags. I bear your secrets and share your sweat, lying patiently in wait. I've never sinned, but still I'm hated and drowned, beaten, then hanged. But the work is never done; I'll rise again in seven days.

Annotation: I'll spin before I'm hung.

209. You should keep it as straight as can be, yet very few do. Most of the time it's slightly bent or curved. Your sadness usually causes it to bend further but don't bend it for too long or it may never be able to fully straighten out again. What is it?

Annotation: Practice keeping it straight every day.

210. What has a spot and is very bright. It can be red, white, blue, yellow or green and it is often blinding.

Annotation: I appear at night if someone trespasses on my property.

211. If Teresa's daughter is my daughter's mother, who am I to Teresa?

Annotation: Read it again and again.

212. In this place, people lie, people cry, and people ask why. In this place, people sleep, people weep, and people's solitude, they keep. What is it?

Annotation: Pay your respects here.

213. Whiling away the hours of flowers. Walking through the fields of gold. Preening and pruning in lights fading hours. For petals to freeze in the cold. What is it?

Annotation: An annual cycle.

214. What can be underwater, under fire, on fire and taking on water all at the same time?

Annotation: I'm equipped with a periscope.

215.   What can be forever wound up but never annoyed?

Annotation: I like to scare to the sound of music.

FIND THE ANSWERS ON THE NEXT PAGE!

201. Wallet.
202. Gator.
203. Umbrella.
204. Hollow.
205. Bagpipes.
206. Soap.
207. He's playing Monopoly.
208. Laundry.
209. Posture.
210. Spotlight.
211. Her daughter.
212. Cemetery.
213. Four seasons.
214. Submarine.
215. Jack In The Box.

216.   I work when I play and I play when I work.

Annotation: I'm very creative.

217.   Why are ghosts good at lying?

Annotation: Harry Potter's cloak.

218.   Why did Mickey Mouse go to Outer space?

Annotation: I'm now considered to be a dwarf planet.

219.   I have wings and I have a tail, across the sky is where I sail. Yet I have no eyes, ears or mouth, and I bob randomly from north to south. What am I?

Annotation: Traditionally, I'm diamond shaped.

220.   A girl is sitting in a house at night that has no lights on at all. There is no lamp, no candle, nothing. Yet she is reading. How?

Annotation: She is feeling too.

221.   What goes around and around the wood, but never goes into the wood?

Annotation: I transport food and water throughout the wood.

222.   A truck driver is going the opposite way to traffic on one-way street. A police officer sees him but doesn't stop him. Why didn't the police officer stop him?

Annotation: The steering wheel has vanished.

223. What kind of money do vampires use?

Annotation: I'm cash obtained through illegal activity.

224. Sometimes I shine, sometimes I am dull, sometimes I am big, and sometimes I am small. I can be pointy, I can be curved, and don't ask me questions because even though I'm sharp, I'm not smart enough to answer you. What am I?

Annotation: I'm a common utensil.

225. What do you get if you add two blackberries and five apples?

Annotation: Think beyond fruit.

226. I can be long and can be short, I can be black, white, brown or purple. You can find me all over the world and I am often the main event. What am I?

Annotation: I'm popular in Asia.

227. I'm an animal named after the animal that I eat, what am I?

Annotation: I have a long snout.

228. I am neither a guest nor a trespasser be, to this place I belong, it belongs also to me.

Annotation: It's where the heart is.

229. I was once full of thoughts but now I'm white and empty. What am I?

Annotation: Find me on the flag of sea robbers.

230. Slayer of regrets, old and new, sought by many, found by few. What am I?

**FIND THE ANSWERS
ON THE
NEXT PAGE!**

216. Musician.
217. Because you can see right through them.
218. Pluto.
219. Kite.
220. The woman is blind, and she is reading braille.
221. The bark on a tree.
222. He isn't driving, he's walking.
223. Blood money.
224. Knife.
225. Lots of gadgets.
226. Rice.
227. Anteater.
228. Home.
229. Skull.
230. Redemption.

231. What does almost no one want, yet almost no one wants to lose?

   Annotation: Study hard to get me.

232. Round like an apple, deep like a cup, yet all the kings horses cannot pull it up. What is it?

   Annotation: Bucket.

233. I have two arms, but fingers none. I have two feet, but cannot run. I carry well, but I have found I carry best with my feet off the ground. What am I?

   Annotation: Find me on a building site.

234. What connects two people but touches only one?

   Annotation: I'm a symbol of a commitment.

235. I start off dry but come out wet. I go in light and come out heavy. What am I?

   Annotation: I contain different types of leaves.

236. What time starts and stops with an "n"?

   Annotation: Find me halfway.

237. What moves without seeing and cries without eyes?

   Annotation: I float through the atmosphere.

238. What is the building that you leave without ever having entered?

Annotation: I hold you at your start.

239.   What goes into the water black and comes out red?

Annotation: I have a hard shell.

240.   I always follow my brother but you cannot see me, only him. You canno
hear him but you can hear me. What are we?

Annotation: We can show up during a storm.

241.   I go up and I go down, towards the sky and ground. I'm present and pas
tense too. Let's go for a ride, me and you. What am I?

Annotation: Find me at the park.

242.   Craig died in Florida. Shortly after, Tracy died at sea. Nobody mourned,
in fact, everyone was absolutely delighted. Why?

Annotation: Are we people?

243.   Flat as a leaf, round as a ring; has two eyes, can't see a thing. What is it'

Annotation: Find me on a garment.

244.   What has three ways out and just one way in?

Annotation: Put it on.

245.   What tree that definitely grows does not have a shadow and does not
grow fruit?

Annotation: This tree can teach you about yourself.

46. What can you share and still have it all for yourself.

   Annotation: Acquire more of it as you learn.

47. Searing 'cross the pitch-black skies. I scream in celebration. Yet moments later, my outburst through, I am naught but imagination.

   Annotation: I'm pyrotechnic.

48. When the horse strokes the cat, the wood begins to sing. What is it?

   Annotation: I begin with a V.

49. A shimmering field that reaches far. Yet it has no tracks, and is crossed without paths. What am I?

   Annotation: I'm divided geographically.

50. Halo of water, tongue of wood, skin of stone, long I've stood. My fingers short reach the sky. Inside my heart men live and die. What is it?

   Annotation: I'm a medieval construct.

FIND THE ANSWERS
ON THE
NEXT PAGE!

231. Their job.
232. Well.
233. Wheelbarrow.
234. Wedding ring.
235. Teabags.
236. Noon.
237. Cloud.
238. The hospital that you were born in.
239. Lobster.
240. Thunder and lightning.
241. See Saw.
242. They were both hurricanes.
243. Button.
244. T-shirt.
245. Family tree.
246. Knowledge.
247. Fireworks.
248. Violin.
249. Ocean.
250. Castle.

251. Sometimes black, sometimes white. I have veins but no blood.

    Annotation: I form in limestone buildings.

252. My legs are knives. I am a knight. I can reclaim what I lose in a fight. What am I?

    Annotation: I'm great with garlic butter sauce.

253. It hold no blessings in disguise. Its rhymes are aims at your demise, it's cast only to ruin, whatever you are doin'.

    Annotation: Maleficent places on Aurora.

254. Its title means "book".

    Annotation: I contain the New and Old Testaments.

255. What has four wings but cannot fly and uses the wind but does not know why?

    Annotation: I convert kinetic energy.

256. A great mysterious place that the bold have been known to journey into.

    Annotation: I begin with the letter U.

257. When the day after tomorrow is yesterday, today will be as far from Wednesday as today was from Wednesday when the day before yesterday was tomorrow. What is the day after this day?

    Annotation: Read carefully!

258. I fly through the air on small feathered wings, seeking out life and destroying all things.

Annotation: I'm an archer's companion.

259. A device for finding furniture in the dark. What am I?

Annotation: Ouch.

260. You'll see savory and stir-fry dishes in Hong Kong sizzling in this. What is it?

Annotation: I begin with the letter W.

261. His big belly supposedly has the ability to dispense good fortune.

Annotation: He was born in Nepal and he died in India.

262. Salty water everywhere but no sea in sight. What am I?

Annotation: I'm a symbol of sorrow.

263. Do what he says and you'll be fine, don't and you lose the game.

Annotation: I'm a popular classroom game.

264. If you're stealing honey, be prepared to be receive vengeance in this form.

Annotation: I begin with the letter S.

265. This is needed for both courage and hardcover books. What is it?

Annotation: It's a series of vertebrae.

FIND THE ANSWERS ON THE NEXT PAGE!

251. Marble.
252. Crab.
253. Curse.
254. Bible.
255. Windmill.
256. Unknown.
257. Thursday.
258. Arrow.
259. Shin.
260. Wok.
261. Buddha.
262. Tears.
263. Simon (Says)
264. Sting.
265. Spine.

266. A circle of stones, never in rows. Stacked one on the other, mystery it sows. What is it?

Annotation: It was founded in the Bronze Age.

267. It is destruction made out of thin air. You hear it howl and give a prayer. Through barns and houses it will tear. It is a deadly funnel of violent and twisting air.
Annotation: I can exceed a speed of 74 mph.

268. Talks like this, a green wise man does. Guess my clue you will.

Annotation: I'm hairy.

269. When it comes in, from sea to shore. Twenty paces you'll see, no less, no more.

Annotation: I'm suspended in the atmosphere.

270. Sharp and long, flag of the world. What is it?

Annotation: The Burj Khalifa.

271. A leathery snake, with a stinging bite. I'll stay coiled up, unless I must fight.

Annotation: I was used to punish.

272. My head bobs lazily in the sun. You think I'm cute. For my face is yellow, my hair is white and my body is green.

Annotation: I begin with the letter D.

273. What table has no legs?

Annotation: Find water on there.

274. It's a game played by serious people that takes place on a global scale.

Annotation: Every country deals with it.

275. It's equally comfortable in an orchestra and a geometry textbook. What is it?

Annotation: Bermuda has a famous one too.

276. Held firmly in the hands, like a sword it cuts deep. Bloodless strokes, all, then forward we leap.

Annotation: This is useful when there is no engine aboard.

277. You are having a bad day if 12 peers deem you to be this. What is it?

Annotation: A verdict.

278. What tastes better than it smells?

Annotation: Think carefully!

279. Thousands of us come together to make a digital image. What are we?

Annotation: We compose memories.

280. What is something that you always have but you always leave behind?

Annotation: Immigration will take them at the airport.

FIND THE ANSWERS ON THE NEXT PAGE!

266. Stonehenge.
267. Hurricane.
268. Yoda.
269. Fog.
270. Tower.
271. Whip.
272. Daisy.
273. Periodic (Table).
274. Politics.
275. Triangle.
276. Paddle.
277. Guilty.
278. Tongue.
279. Pixels.
280. Fingerprints.

281.   I am nothing but holes tied to holes, yet I'm as strong as iron.

Annotation: I shackle prisoners.

282.   What is never used unless it's in a tight place?

Annotation: It's also the name of a city in Ireland.

283.   The greatest nemesis of lactose intolerant. What is it?

Annotation: A farm.

284.   Both old people and owls are said to be possessing this trait.

Annotation: Gain more as you age.

285.   What type of paper can you neither read nor write on?

Annotation: I like the beach.

286.   Iron roof, glass walls, burns and burns and never fails.

Annotation: I guide through the darkness.

287.   What do you have when you're sitting down that you don't have when you're standing up.

Annotation: Santa Claus invites you to sit on his.

288.   Known to accessorise with feathers, trumpets, and harps. What is it?

Annotation: It's a spiritual being.

89. What travels from house to house and is sometimes narrow and sometimes wide but always stays outside?

Annotation: I lead the way.

90. Never alive but practically extinct. How we miss the letters pressing the ribbon of ink. What is it?

Annotation: Personal computers overtook me.

91. It is by nature, soft as silk; a puffy cloud, white as milk; snow tops this tropical crop; the dirtiest part of a mop.

Annotation: I precede the word candy.

92. What bird can lift the heaviest weight?

Annotation: I'm also a piece of machinery found on a building site.

93. Describes universities like Harvard and can be poisonous.

Annotation: I'm a Eurasian plant.

94. Autumn leaves and bad ten-pin bowlers wreak havoc on this. What is it?

Annotation: I begin with the letter G.

95. A beacon from home to guide your way. It can be a lifesaver on a stormy day. What is it

Annotation: I help struggling ships.

96. Looks like water, but it's heat. Sits on sand, lays on concrete. A play on the eyes, but it's all lies.

Annotation: See me in the desert.

297. Though I wonder the earth, I am no longer here. I am pale and I chill everyone near. Who am I?

Annotation: I'm an apparition.

298. What kind of room has no doors or windows?

Annotation: I taste delicious.

299. What is the center of gravity?

Annotation: Look closely!

300. Can you name two days starting with T, besides Tuesday and Thursday?

Annotation: Good luck!

FIND THE ANSWERS ON THE NEXT PAGE!

281. Chains.
282. Cork.
283. Dairy.
284. Wisdom.
285. Sandpaper.
286. Lantern.
287. Lap.
288. Angel
289. Path.
290. Typewriter.
291. Cotton.
292. Crane.
293. Ivy.
294. Gutter.
295. Lighthouse.
296. Mirage.
297. Ghost.
298. A mush-room.
299. The letter V.
300. Today and Tomorrow.

One Last Thing

If you have enjoyed this book, please don't forget to write a **review** of this publication. It is really useful feedback as well as providing untold encouragement to the author.

Made in the USA
Coppell, TX
07 November 2020

40919118R00060